Comparing Refugees and South Africans in the Urban Informal Sector

Jonathan Crush, Godfrey Tawodzera, Cameron McCordic
and Sujata Ramachandran

SAMP MIGRATION POLICY SERIES NO. 78

Series Editor: Prof. Jonathan Crush

Southern African Migration Programme (SAMP)
2017

AUTHORS

Jonathan Crush is the CIGI Chair in Global Migration and Development at the Balsillie School of International Affairs, Waterloo, Canada.

Godfrey Tawodzera is a Senior Lecturer in the Department of Geography and Environmental Studies, University of Limpopo, Polokwane, South Africa.

Cameron McCordic is a Post-Doctoral Fellow at the Balsillie School of International Affairs.

Sujata Ramachandran is a Senior Researcher at the Southern African Migration Programme.

ACKNOWLEDGEMENT

The research for this report was funded by the UNHCR (Geneva).

© Southern African Migration Programme (SAMP) 2017

Published by the Southern African Migration Programme, International Migration Research Centre, Balsillie School of International Affairs, Waterloo, Ontario, Canada samponline.org

First published 2017

ISBN 978-1-920596-38-5

Cover photo by Thom Pierce: Zimbabwean entrepreneur Lorraine Moyo

Production by Bronwen Dachs Muller, Cape Town

Printed by The Printing Press, Cape Town

CONTENTS   PAGE

LIST OF TABLES

LIST OF FIGURES

EXECUTIVE SUMMARY

This report systematically compares over 2,000 South African and non-South African informal sector entrepreneurs and assesses the similarities and differences between them in terms of their business operations and their business risks. The two comparison groups are (i) refugees (holders of Section 24 permits) in Cape Town and Limpopo and (ii) South African migrants operating businesses in the same localities.

The general literature on informal entrepreneurship conventionally divides participants into survival (or necessity) entrepreneurs and opportunity entrepreneurs. The former are driven to participate by the need to survive and because they have no other choice. The latter choose to work in the informal sector because they see opportunities for economic advancement, they prefer to work for themselves rather than for others, or they feel that they have the right aptitude. In the South African context, studies of entrepreneurial motivation in the informal sector have sought to go beyond the idea of survivalism and demonstrate that many participants in the informal economy are not driven by desperation but are highly motivated entrepreneurs. This survey used an entrepreneurial motivation scale to assess differences, if any, between South Africans and refugees. The ranking of reasons for starting a business does not differ significantly within each group but there are important differences between them. Economic survival motivations scored most highly for both groups, and providing employment or a service to others was the least important. The highest single factor for both groups was the need to earn more money for basic needs. Also very important for both was the desire to provide family with greater financial security and the desire to make more money to remit to family at home. In other words, financial support of dependants is a strong motivating factor for informal sector entrepreneurship.

In terms of the differences between the two groups of informal sector entrepreneurs, there were several important findings:

- South Africans scored higher than refugees on only two motivational factors: "I was unemployed and unable to find a job" and "I had a job but it did not pay enough." This suggests that for South African migrants, informal sector participation is more closely tied to the absence of formal employment than it is for refugees. Statistically, refugee entrepreneurs have about 50% lower odds of starting their business because of being unable to find a job, which may simply be a reflection of the fact that refugees are shut out of the formal labour market and do not even try to find employment there.

- Refugees were much more likely to be motivated by a desire to provide a service or product to South Africans and to contribute to the development of South Africa. Indeed, refugees had four times the odds of desiring to contribute to the development of South Africa than South Africans.

- Refugees could count on the help and support of others to a much greater degree than South Africans. Refugees had three times the odds of stressing the importance of obtaining help from others in starting their business and going into partnership with others.

- Refugees were consistently more positive about their personal aptitude for running a business. On a series of personal attributes associated with entrepreneurship, refugees had two to three times the odds of having these characteristics.

- On average, South Africans have been in business for longer than refugees with 19% of South African and only 2% of refugee businesses established before 2000. In total, 61% of refugee businesses and 44% of South African businesses were established after 2010.

- Only 9% of South Africans and 18% of refugees were operating an informal business before migrating. This does not suggest a massive competitive advantage conferred by prior experience. Over 80% of the refugee entrepreneurs were not operating an informal sector business prior to migrating to South Africa. The stereotypical idea that refugees somehow have business "in their blood" is therefore not supported by the evidence of this survey.

- Three-quarters of enterprises run by both refugees and South African migrants are located in the retail sector. However, the two groups tend to occupy and dominate different market niches. South Africans are more strongly represented in food retail. Around 70% of the entrepreneurs selling fresh produce and cooked food were South Africans. On the other hand, over 70% of those selling most types of personal and household products were refugees. In the service sector, refugees dominate hair cutting and braiding, as well as car repairs and IT. South Africans tend to dominate shoe repairs, transportation and car washing and guarding.

- Statistically, the South African entrepreneurs had almost twice the odds of running a business established before 2011, almost 10 times the odds of starting a business with less than ZAR5,000 and almost seven times the odds of currently running a business valued at less than ZAR5,000, which does suggest that for reasons unrelated to prior experience, refugees tend to run higher value businesses and grow them more effectively.

These findings led to a comparative analysis of the business strategies of the two groups to see whether there were significant differences between them and which contributes more to the economy. The first point of comparison concerns business location. In the case of Cape Town, there are areas of the city where each group tends to dominate: refugee businesses are more common in the CBD and Bellville, for instance, while South Africans are more commonly located along transport routes in and out of the city (such as on streets and at taxi ranks and bus terminals). Half of the South Africans operate stalls on roadsides and 21% at taxi ranks. This compares with only 31% and 2% of refugees respectively. The other major difference is that half of the refugees operate from a fixed shop or workshop, compared to only 8% of the South Africans. When compared with the refugee entrepreneurs, the South African migrant entrepreneurs had greater odds of choosing a business location based on it having the greatest number of potential customers, tradition, cost of land, and fewer police in the area. The refugees had higher odds of choosing their business location based on the other locational factors, especially access to services, property rentals, safety concerns, and distance from competitors.

Second, refugee entrepreneurs were much more likely than South Africans to rent their business premises. Almost 60% paid rent to a South African landlord. Another 13% paid rent to the municipality (as did 10% of the South Africans). Nearly 50% of South Africans operated their businesses rent free (compared to only 5% of refugees). What this means is that around three-quarters of South Africans do not pay any rent for their premises, while over 80% of refugees do. The refugee entrepreneurs also pay a higher monthly rent, on average, than those South Africans who do pay rent (ZAR4,000 per month versus ZAR2,820 per month). In effect, many South Africans are able to augment their household income through renting business premises to refugees and therefore benefit from their presence.

Third, there is a common assumption that the strategies adopted by refugees give them a strong competitive advantage over South Africans. The South Africans had higher odds of adjusting their operating hours according to customer numbers and purchasing insurance. Both had roughly equal odds of offering credit to customers. However, refugees had significantly higher odds of keeping business records, selling goods more cheaply than competitors, purchasing in bulk with others and negotiating prices with suppliers. The final point of business strategy comparison concerns hiring practices. Almost half of the refugee entrepreneurs have paid employees compared to only 21% of the South Africans. The refugees in this sample provided three times as many jobs as the South Africans. However, refugee and South African enterprises create jobs for South Africans at roughly the same rate.

In terms of business risks, the official government stance towards violent attacks on migrant businesses is that they are the actions of fringe criminal elements. If mere criminality is the problem, we might expect South Africans operating in the same areas to be equally affected and some researchers have claimed just that. They argue that the attacks on informal businesses in South Africa are structural in nature, shaped by competition and other localized factors rather than xenophobia. To them, some combination of criminality and economic competition explains the violence. This report takes issue with this conclusion, demonstrating that while South Africans are not immune, refugees are more vulnerable and that xenophobia needs to be reintroduced as an explanatory factor:

- Comparing the security risks of the two groups, it is clear that South Africans are not immune from any of these risks. Nearly a third had been robbed of their stock and nearly 20% had had income stolen. The degree of vulnerability to other security risks was much lower. Therefore, while South Africans in the informal sector are also victims of crime, there is no support for the contention that South Africans and non-South Africans are equally at risk or victimized.

- On every count, the proportion of refugees affected by a security risk was higher, sometimes significantly so. For example, 21% had been victims of attacks or assaults, compared to 4% of South Africans. Also, 19% had been harassed or extorted by the police, compared to 6% of South Africans. Some 38% had been victims of theft of income, compared to 19% of South Africans.

- Statistical analysis showed that South African entrepreneurs had lower odds of experiencing all potential risks on the list. Refugees were nearly three times as likely to be victims of theft of income and five times as likely to be subject to demands for bribes by police. The odds of a refugee entrepreneur being physically assaulted, experiencing prejudice, and being arrested and detained were over five times higher than for South Africans.

- In theory, we might expect to see higher degrees of informal business security risks for both groups in large cities such as Cape Town compared to the much smaller towns of Limpopo. For both groups, Limpopo was indeed safer than Cape Town. For example,

56% of refugees and 31% of South Africans had experienced theft of goods in Cape Town. In Limpopo, the equivalent figures were 38% and 30%, a much lower spread than in Cape Town. In both locations, however, the risks are significantly higher for refugees than South Africans. Indeed, refugees in Limpopo were more vulnerable than South Africans in both Limpopo and Cape Town.

- Another common belief is that security risks are higher in informal settlements than in other parts of the city, particularly as many of the reports of violence against businesses come from informal settlements, where general crime levels are much higher. For both refugees and South Africans operating businesses in informal settlements, the security risks are higher across almost all indicators. However, the difference in the degree of risk between refugees and South Africans is significantly greater in informal settlements than it is in formal areas of the city. The only indicator where formal areas are riskier for both is in the chances of having goods confiscated by the police.

- Refugees were far more likely than South Africans to say that their business operations had been negatively affected by xenophobia: 38% versus 5%. There are two possible reasons for South Africans being affected: first, when collective xenophobic violence occurs at a particular localized settlement, it is possible that some South African-owned businesses may be caught up in the looting and vandalism. A second explanation is that there are cascading, spillover effects on South African small businesses with cooperative, dependent relationships and linkages with affected migrant-operated businesses.

This report set out to systematically compare the informal enterprises established by different categories of migrant in South African urban areas. This comparative analysis of refugees and internal migrants suggests that there is a need for much greater nuance in policy and academic discussions about the impact of refugee migration on the South African informal economy. The stereotyping of refugees in public discourse as undermining and destroying South African competitors is far removed from the reality. While refugees seem able to access greater amounts of start-up capital (although neither they nor South Africans can access bank loans), both groups seem able to grow their businesses. Partly this is because they tend to occupy different niches in the informal economy with South Africans focused on the food sector and refugees on services and retailing household goods. This may help to explain another difference between the two with refugees tending to patronize wholesalers for their supplies and South Africans purchasing from supermarkets and fresh produce markets.

The idea promulgated by government that refugees have a competitive advantage as in-their-blood entrepreneurs is clearly fallacious. Despite South Africa's liberal refugee legislation, restrictive employment policies mean that working for, and then establishing, an informal enterprise is virtually the only available livelihood option. But to argue that refugees come to South Africa with pre-existing skills and business experience is misplaced. Refugees, like small-business owners everywhere, are extremely motivated and hard-working. They employ several business strategies to achieve monetary success, although expansion is hampered by the need to support dependants in South Africa and the home country, which limits reinvestment of profits in the business. These strategies are not illegal or even underhand but quite transparent and could be emulated.

This report shows that the general effect of operating small businesses in the informal economic sector does make business owners of all kinds vulnerable, but this alone cannot explain the greater vulnerabilities of the refugee cohort. Instead, xenophobia and their status as "outsiders" adds another layer of risks for such operators. Limited access to police protection and mistreatment by officers only exacerbates this insecurity. Refugees themselves are in no doubt that they are singled out and that it is xenophobia that drives the violence and harassment they experience.

INTRODUCTION

In 2014, South Africa's Minister of Small Business Development, Lindiwe Zulu, made a public comparison between South African and migrant informal entrepreneurs, echoing popular misconceptions about both groups. She suggested that South African business owners were largely inept and should learn from the business practices of their foreign counterparts who were "better at running shops than the local owners."[1] At the same time, South Africans were at a natural disadvantage because they had no history of entrepreneurship. The reason for refugee success, she continued, is that business "is in their blood… from the moment they are born, they are introduced to trade. Their mothers, uncles, everyone trades." As a result, they "operate in the same communities in which we fail."[2] These stereotypical comparisons are echoed in the research literature. There is a common idea in the business literature, for example, that poor black South Africans lack entrepreneurial ambition and that this helps to explain the relatively small size of the South African informal economy and the high rate of local informal business failure.[3]

Another conventional wisdom is that "survivalist" South Africans in the informal economy are being displaced by "entrepreneurial" migrants.[4] South Africans supposedly display a "survivalist mentality and one dimensional [business] strategy" leading to poorer performance than migrants.[5] A comparison of South African and Somali *spaza* shop owners in Cape Town found that the latter scored better on various indicators of entrepreneurial orientation including achievement, innovation, personal initiative and autonomy.[6] In addition, migrant businesses grew faster and created more jobs than South African businesses. By contrast, some have suggested that business failure is not inevitable and that South African survivalists can grow their enterprises and create jobs.[7] Other studies have suggested that the gap between South African and migrant entrepreneurs is not as wide as is commonly supposed. One study of 500 retail enterprises in Gauteng, for example, found that motivations to start a business did not differ significantly between South Africans and immigrants.[8] A study of street traders in inner-city Johannesburg concluded that South Africans were actually more innovative than migrants, although they did not display the same levels of proactiveness and competitive aggression.[9] While migrant traders had earned more than their South African counterparts in 2008 and 2010, in 2009 the South Africans were the higher earners.[10]

The sustainability of all informal enterprises is shaped by the challenges they encounter and the manner in which they are able to manage business risks effectively. A sizeable body of research has shown that all small enterprises in the South African informal economy face significant business obstacles, preventing them from maximizing their potential.[11] These business risks include limited trading spaces; lack of access to loans from formal financial institutions; few technical, financial and business-related skills; excessive licensing or regulatory restrictions on business operations; lack of a well-defined policy framework for operating; intense competition with other similar businesses; and lack of infrastructure such as adequate storage facilities.[12]

In South Africa, business risks are compounded by security risks because of the unpredictable and often dangerous operating environment. These security risks are of several main types. In many cities, the informal economy is regarded with suspicion and even outright hostility by municipalities, and seen as a reservoir of crime and illegality.[13] The resulting oppressive regulatory environment is enforced by the South African Police Services (SAPS) and municipal police who make regular raids, issue fines, and confiscate goods.[14] Harassment by police and enforcement officials is compounded by police misconduct including demands for bribes and illegal confiscation of business inventory and stock. Informal businesses are regular targets of national (Operation Fiela), provincial (Operation Hardstick in Limpopo) and city-wide (Operation Cleansweep in Johannesburg) police purges of the streets and large-scale seizure of stock. The courts have generally concluded that these operations are largely targeted at the foreign-owned businesses. A 2014 Supreme Court judgment striking down Operation Hardstick, for example, left the court with "the uneasy feeling that the stance adopted by the authorities in relation to the licensing of *spaza* shops and tuck-shops was in order to induce foreign nationals who were destitute to leave our shores."[15] The obverse of police misconduct is a failure to provide consistent protection when businesses are under threat or are victims of crime and other violence.

Many informal businesses service the basic needs of low-income, crime-ridden communities. This means that, by definition, they are vulnerable to opportunistic and often violent crime in the form of theft, robbery and assault. There is also a clear pattern of escalating mob violence in many parts of the country which is increasingly directed at informal businesses.[16] Nationwide mob violence and looting in May 2008 and early 2015 were the most high-profile examples but in the years between and since there have been numerous more localized attacks. These assaults generally involve widespread looting, destruction and burning of property, and physical assault and murder. There is considerable evidence that this form of violence is targeted almost exclusively at foreign-owned businesses and cannot therefore be easily dismissed as non-xenophobic.

The official government stance towards xenophobic attacks has shifted from a lack of acknowledgement of xenophobia's presence to public denial of its very existence in the country.[17] Instead, the attacks are consistently written off as the actions of fringe criminal elements. If mere criminality is the source of the plague of chronic violence against non-South African entrepreneurs, however, we might expect South Africans operating in the same areas to be equally affected. Some researchers claim that this is indeed the case.[18] They argue that the attacks on informal businesses in South Africa are structural in nature, shaped by competition and localized factors other than nationality or xenophobia. One study of Delft in Cape Town maintains that "despite a recent history of intense economic competition in the *spaza* market in which foreign shopkeepers have come to dominate, levels of violent crime against foreign shopkeepers…are not significantly higher than against South African shopkeepers."[19] They conclude that there is no need to invoke xenophobia to explain violence against non-South African informal enterprises. Rather, "some combination of criminality and economic competition seems to explain the violence."[20]

A larger study by the same authors examines patterns of violence in three cities and concludes that "it simply is not true that…South African shopkeepers experience less violent crime than foreign shopkeepers" and therefore that "the chance of being violently targeted is less about nationality, and more about whether you keep prices low and (presumably) profits high."[21] The question to be addressed is whether these security risks – government purges, police misconduct, opportunistic crime and mob violence – affect South Africans and non-South African informal businesses with equal intensity. If we accept the argument that xenophobia is not a factor, then we would expect there to be no difference between the frequency and severity with which the two groups are affected. If, however, there is systematic evidence that these attacks are experienced more severely by non-South African migrant informal business owners, then xenophobia needs to be reintroduced as an explanatory factor.

METHODOLOGY

This report systematically compares a group of South African and non-South African informal sector entrepreneurs and assesses the similarities and differences between them, both in terms of their business operations and their business risks. The two comparison groups are (i) refugees (holders of Section 24 permits) in Cape Town and Limpopo and (ii) South African migrants operating businesses in the same localities. Without a census or register of informal sector businesses to create a sampling frame, an alternative strategy was used to ensure a degree of representativeness of the samples. Two procedures were adopted: (a) maximum variation sampling (MVS) to identify a sub-set of areas within the city (in the case of Cape Town and a sub-set of towns in Limpopo) in which to conduct the research; and (b) random sampling of the population within the selected research sites. MVS is based on the principle of maximum diversity, an extension of the statistical principle of regression towards the mean where instead of seeking representativeness through equal probability it is sought by including a broad range of extremes. The precise application of MVS follows that used in a study of the informal sector in Bangalore, India.[22]

Five different types of area in Cape Town were selected: commercial, formal residential, informal residential, mixed formal and informal residential, and industrial. Within each of these types, contrasting and geographically separated research sites were selected in the commercial (two sites), industrial (two sites), formal residential (three sites) informal settlements (three sites) and mixed formal and informal residential (two sites). In the case of Limpopo, the primary criterion for the application of "maximum variation sampling" was urban size. Six towns, covering a wide size range and scattered around the province, were selected. In each research site, the same systematic sampling approach was adopted. This approach is feasible because the survey was conducted in urban areas where houses and businesses are located along streets. Sampling was therefore conducted along street lines in each site, the mapped grid-pattern exhibited by streets was utilized, sampling one street after the other in successive fashion moving from west to east. After identifying the first five enterprises on a street, and randomly selecting the first of the five for the sample, every third enterprise was selected thereafter. Provided the enterprise was owned by a local (a South African migrant defined as someone born outside the city or province) or someone with refugee status (Section 24), the enterprise qualified for inclusion in the study. The process was repeated in each survey site. Where business owners were not available for interview, field workers made three call backs to the enterprise, after which a substitution was made. The number of refugee and South African entrepreneurs interviewed in each site is shown in Tables 1 and 2.

TABLE 1: Location of Interviews in Cape Town

	Refugees	South Africans
Bellville	91	84
CBD	103	88
Delft	26	43
Imizamo Yethu	34	18
Khayelitsha	25	23
Maitland	40	10
Masiphumelele	10	34
Parow	82	24
Philippi	21	42
Dunoon	42	93
Nyanga	3	31
Observatory	27	12
Total surveyed	504	502

TABLE 2: Location of Interviews in Limpopo

	Refugees	South Africans
Polokwane	159	166
Musina	121	74
Louis Trichardt	36	51
Thohoyandou	59	57
Burgersfort	96	41
Tzaneen	33	177
Total surveyed	504	566

In total, the survey drew a sample of 1,068 South African entrepreneurs and 1,008 refugee entrepreneurs. For the purposes of this comparative analysis, the report combines the two sub-groups of refugees (in Cape Town and Limpopo) into one group and does the same with the South Africans.

COMPARING ENTREPRENEURIAL MOTIVATION

South Africans and refugees appear to face very different livelihood prospects in the country's urban areas. Although South Africa does not have a refugee encampment policy and refugees are permitted, by law, to pursue employment, there is much evidence to suggest that they face considerable barriers in accessing the formal labour market.[23] They have been shut out of the security industry (where many were initially employed) and face substantial hurdles in getting employers to accept their documentation. South Africans, on the other hand, should theoretically have none of these problems but they face other barriers including limited skills and training, and high rates of unemployment (currently around 30% nationally and as high as 45% amongst urban youth).[24] South African migrants to the cities often end up living in informal settlements far from formal job opportunities and also have to compete in the job market with long-time residents of the city who have a significant geographical and networking advantage. For both sets of migrants, then, the informal economy is often the only livelihood niche they can find.

The general literature on informal entrepreneurship conventionally divides participants into survival (or necessity) entrepreneurs and opportunity entrepreneurs.[25] The former are driven to participate by the need to survive and because they have no other choice. The latter choose to work in the informal sector because they see opportunities for economic advancement, or they prefer to work for themselves rather than for others, or they feel that they have the right aptitude. Distinguishing between these two types of entrepreneur and their likely differences in entrepreneurial motivation and orientation has generated a large empirical and methodological literature. In the South African context, studies of entrepreneurial motivation have sought to go beyond the idea of survivalism and demonstrate that many participants in the informal economy are not driven there out of desperation but are highly motivated entrepreneurs.[26]

One of the most common ways of deciding what lies behind personal decisions to establish an informal enterprise is to measure entrepreneurial motivation. This involves the development of possible reasons why the informal enterprise was started and then asking respondents to rank them on a Likert scale from 1 (no importance) to 5 (extremely important). Both refugees and South African migrants were presented with 24 possibilities to rate. A mean score was calculated for each group on each statement (Table 3). For ease of interpretation, we have grouped the 24 statements under four main themes (a) economic survival; (b) provision of employment or a service to others; (c) business experience and appeal; and (d) entrepreneurial orientation. Two things immediately stand out from a descriptive comparison of means. First, both refugees and migrants tend to assign the same relative importance to each of the 24 factors, which might suggest that they have a similar motivational profile. The second notable finding is that almost across the board, even on statements that had a low mean score, refugees' scores were higher than South African migrants. This could indicate a greater general degree of commitment to participation in the informal economy amongst refugees.

TABLE 3: Entrepreneurial Motivation of Refugees and South Africans

	South Africans (mean score)	Refugees (mean score)
Economic survival/financial support of dependants		
I needed more money just to survive	4.10	4.31
I wanted to give my family greater financial security	3.69	3.97
I was unemployed and unable to find a job	3.43	2.89
I wanted to make more money to send to my family in my home area/country	3.00	3.57
I had a job but it did not pay enough	2.29	2.24
I had a job but it did not suit my qualifications and experience	1.44	1.62
Providing employment/product/service		
I wanted to provide a product/service to South Africans	2.74	3.41
I wanted to contribute to the development of South Africa	2.69	3.35
I wanted to provide a service/product to non-South Africans/migrants and refugees	2.46	3.00
I wanted to provide employment for people from my home area/country	1.93	2.25
I wanted to provide employment for members of my family	2.19	2.27
I wanted to provide employment for other South Africans	2.10	2.29
Business experience/appeal		
I wanted more control over my own time/to be my own boss	3.08	3.72
I have always wanted to run my own business	3.06	3.75
Support and help in starting my business was available from other South Africans/refugees	2.05	3.03
I decided to go into business in partnership with others	1.62	2.37
My family has always been involved in business	1.81	2.34

Entrepreneurial orientation		
I have the right personality to run my own business	3.01	3.45
I wanted to do something new and challenging	2.83	3.34
I like to learn new skills	2.83	3.41
I enjoy taking risks	2.73	3.24
I like to challenge myself	2.84	3.37
I wanted to increase my status in the community	2.48	2.99
I wanted to compete with others and be the best	2.48	3.07

The only two factors on which South Africans scored higher than refugees were: "I was unemployed and unable to find a job" and "I had a job but it did not pay enough." This suggests that for South African migrants, informal sector participation is more closely tied to the absence of formal employment than it is for refugees. Of the four groups of factors, economic survival motivations scored most highly for both groups, and providing an employment or service was the least important. The highest single factor for both groups was the need for more money to survive (both with means over 4.0). Also very important for both was the desire to provide family with greater financial security and the desire to make more money to remit to family at home. In other words, financial support of dependants is a strong motivating factor for informal sector entrepreneurship. Neither group was highly motivated by a desire to provide employment for others but refugees were much more likely to be motivated by a desire to provide a service or product to South Africans (3.41 versus 2.74) and to contribute to the development of South Africa (3.35 versus 2.69).

Although both groups said that wanting to run their own business and be their own boss was important to them, the refugees scored significantly higher on both factors. One of the major differences between the two was the amount of help and support they could count on from others, with refugees scoring much higher than South Africans (3.03 versus 2.05). Refugees were also consistently more positive about their personal aptitude for running a business. This is clear in the grouping of entrepreneurial orientation factors where refugees scored above 3.0 on six of the seven factors compared to South Africans who scored above 3.0 on only one.

While these frequency distributions tell an interesting story about the differences and similarities between South African migrant and refugee entrepreneurs, it is difficult to gauge their statistical significance. The main challenge is that the dependent variable for the comparison (the importance ranking for each variable) is at an ordinal level of measurement with varying distributions across each sampled group. This means that we need to use non-parametric tests of difference and bin the motivation factors into binary level indicators. Each indicator was therefore assigned two values: not important (1 in the original scale) and important (2-5 in the original scale). A combination of odds ratio calculations and Pearson's chi-square test of independence were used to test for significance. The odds ratio calculations show how migrant status is associated with a change in the odds of ranking each motivation factor (where a value greater than 1 indicates increased odds and less than 1 indicates decreased odds). These calculations are supported by 95% confidence intervals and the p-values taken from a chi-square analysis (where an alpha of 0.05 is used as a threshold for a statistically significant difference in the distribution of scores across the two groups) (Table 4).

TABLE 4: Odds Ratio Calculations of Motivational Factors

Entrepreneurial motivation factor	Odds ratio	95% confidence interval		Pearson chi-square	Df	P-value (2-sided)
		Lower	Upper			
I was unemployed and unable to find a job**	0.496	0.411	0.599	54.036	1	<.001
I had a job but it did not pay enough	1.012	0.851	1.204	.019	1	0.895
I had a job but it did not suit my qualifications and experience**	1.631	1.322	2.012	21.088	1	<.001
I wanted to provide employment for members of my family**	1.344	1.128	1.600	10.970	1	0.001
I wanted to provide employment for people from my home area/country**	1.840	1.540	2.198	45.499	1	<.001
I wanted to provide employment for other South Africans**	1.597	1.341	1.902	27.682	1	<.001
I needed more money just to survive**	1.770	1.275	2.457	11.880	1	0.001
I wanted to give my family greater financial security**	1.651	1.294	2.105	16.483a	1	<.001
I wanted to make more money to send to my family in my home area/country**	2.942	2.393	3.618	109.114a	1	<.001
I decided to go into business in partnership with others**	2.931	2.423	3.545	126.855	1	<.001

Support and help in starting my business was available from other South Africans/refugees**	3.155	2.635	3.778	160.774	1	<.001
My family has always been involved in business**	2.149	1.793	2.575	69.422a	1	<.001
I wanted to provide a service/product to non-South Africans/migrants and refugees**	2.085	1.741	2.496	64.788	1	<.001
I wanted to provide a product/service to South Africans**	2.550	2.103	3.093	92.934	1	<.001
I have always wanted to run my own business**	2.806	2.268	3.471	94.245	1	<.001
I have the right personality to run my own business**	2.176	1.787	2.650	61.018	1	<.001
I wanted to do something new and challenging**	2.289	1.890	2.772	73.209	1	<.001
I like to learn new skills**	2.590	2.128	3.153	92.620	1	<.001
I enjoy taking risks**	2.299	1.901	2.781	75.044	1	<.001
I like to challenge myself**	2.466	2.028	2.998	83.975	1	<.001
I wanted more control over my own time/to be my own boss**	2.887	2.331	3.574	98.785	1	<.001
I wanted to increase my status in the community**	2.193	1.832	2.626	74.095	1	<.001
I wanted to compete with others and be the best**	2.581	2.151	3.096	106.434	1	<.001
I wanted to contribute to the development of South Africa**	3.677	3.001	4.505	166.788	1	<.001

* p<.05 on both Pearson's chi-square and Fisher's exact test

** p<.01 on both Pearson's chi-square and Fisher's exact test

Note: Odds ratios measure change in odds from South African to refugee entrepreneurs

The major conclusions from the analysis are as follows: first, refugee entrepreneurs had about 50% lower odds of starting their business because of being unable to find a job. Second, refugees had almost four times the odds of desiring to contribute to the development of South Africa and three times the odds of stressing the importance of obtaining help from others in starting their business and going into partnership with others. Third, refugees had nearly three time the odds of starting a business with the intention of remitting money to family at home. Finally, refugees had two to three times the odds of assigning importance to the range of personal entrepreneurial orientation factors.

CONTRASTING BUSINESS PROFILES

The survey highlighted a number of similarities and differences in the informal business activities of refugee and South African migrant enterprises. First, more South Africans had been in business for a longer period of time (Table 5 and Figure 1). For example, 19% of the South African businesses were established before 2000, compared to only 2% of the refugee businesses. However, the majority of all businesses were started in the past decade with 61% of refugee businesses and 44% of South African businesses established after 2010. This finding is certainly consistent with the general perception that refugees have been entering the informal economy in growing numbers.

TABLE 5: Year of Business Establishment

Year	South Africans		Refugees	
	No.	%	No.	%
<= 1990	46	4.4	1	0.1
1991-1995	49	4.7	1	0.1
1996-2000	115	11.0	18	1.8
2001-2005	124	11.9	70	7.1
2006-2010	246	23.6	293	29.6
2011-2016	462	44.3	608	61.4
Total	1,042	100.0	991	100.0

FIGURE 1: Year of Business Establishment

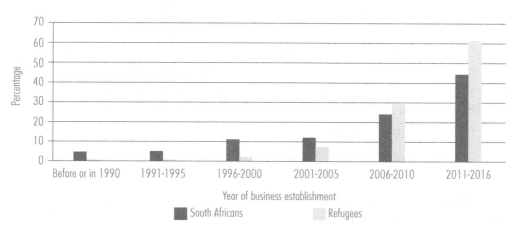

Second, since both groups are migrants to the city, it is important to see if they go into business as soon as they arrive or if business start-up comes later. Only 32% of refugees and 21% of South Africans started a business within the first year of arrival (Table 6). This general pattern of a greater time lapse on the part of the South Africans is further demonstrated by the fact that 41% of them started their business within two years of arrival, compared to 61% of the refugees. Both groups have similar numbers who waited three to 10 years but starting a business after 10 years or more was definitely a South African preserve (at 24% compared to 3% of refugees). The general time lapse in both groups indicates that immediate start-up is not an option for most. Both tend to work first in the formal or informal economy, often to raise the start-up capital to branch out on their own.

TABLE 6: Time Lapse Between Year of Migration and Business Start-Up

Years	South Africans		Refugees	
	No.	%	No.	%
0	213	21.4	304	32.0
1-2	196	19.7	277	29.2
3-5	173	17.4	201	21.2
6-10	172	17.3	140	14.7
>10	242	24.3	28	2.9

Third, it is theoretically possible that the shorter time-lag between migration and start-up amongst refugees is also because they have prior business experience. The respondents were all asked what their main occupation was prior to leaving their home country or area. Only 9% of the South Africans said that they were operating their own informal sector business. The figure for refugees was higher, at 18%, but this does not suggest a massive competitive advantage conferred by prior experience. More than 80% of the refugee entrepreneurs were not operating an informal sector business before migrating to South Africa. The stereotypical idea that refugees somehow have business "in their blood" is therefore not supported by the evidence of this survey.

Fourth, the survey found that the majority of enterprises of both refugees and South African migrants are located in the retail sector (Table 7). A small number of businesses (9% of refugees and 6% of South Africans) are involved in more than one sector; for example, a business that manufactured and sold arts and crafts would count as both a retail and manufacturing enterprise. Or a business offering a service, such as a hair salon, may also be involved in selling products. At this sectoral level of analysis, it appears that there is potential for significant intra-sectoral competition between the two groups. However, if the activity profile is disaggregated, the picture is more nuanced (Table 8).

TABLE 7: Sectors of Informal Business Operation

Sector	South Africans		Refugees	
	No.	%	No.	%
Retail, trade and wholesale	828	77.5	778	77.2
Services	262	24.5	271	26.9
Manufacturing	41	3.8	60	6.0
Other	4	0.4	2	0.2
Note: Multiple response question				

TABLE 8: Main Goods and Services Provided

	% of total enterprises owned by South Africans	% of total enterprises owned by refugees	% of South African enterprises selling product or service	% of refugee enterprises selling product or service
Retail				
Food and beverages				
Fruit and vegetables	27.1	13.4	68.2	31.8
Cooked food (ready to eat)	18.4	6.7	74.3	25.7
Confectionary	17.5	17.0	52.2	47.8
Cool drinks/pop/canned drinks	13.1	22.3	38.4	61.6
Livestock (e.g. chickens)	1.7	0.2	90.0	10.0
Alcohol	0.9	0.4	71.4	28.6
Personal and household goods				
Cigarettes	13.3	19.9	40.8	59.2
Clothing and footwear	7.7	19.5	29.4	70.6
Accessories (bags, sunglasses)	6.1	16.5	28.1	71.9
Toiletries and cosmetics	3.9	14.8	22.0	78.0

Household products	3.4	9.3	27.7	72.3
Electronics	1.8	7.5	20.0	80.0
CDs/DVDs	1.1	2.6	31.6	68.4
Books/newspapers	0.7	2.9	19.4	80.6
Other goods				
Arts and crafts	1.1	2.6	31.6	68.4
Hardware/tools	1.1	2.2	35.3	64.7
Car parts	0.5	0.5	50.0	50.0
Other	15.3	14.2	53.2	46.8
Services				
Haircutting and braiding	6.4	15.1	30.9	69.1
Car washing	3.4	0.4	90.0	10.0
Car parking/guarding	2.3	0.0	100.0	0.0
Shoe repairs	2.0	0.7	75.0	25.0
Car repairs	1.2	0.5	27.8	72.2
Telephone	1.2	1.6	44.8	55.2
IT/internet	0.9	2.7	27.0	73.0
Transportation (taxi/passengers)	0.5	0.2	71.4	0.2
Rentals	0.4	0.1	80.0	20.0
Financial (loans)	0.3	0.1	75.0	25.0
Accommodation	0.2	0.2	50.0	50.0
Construction (building)	0.2	0.0	100.0	0.0
Traditional doctor	0.2	0.2	50.0	50.0
Transportation (goods)	0.2	0.1	66.6	33.4
Medicine (pharmacy)	0.1	0.1	50.0	50.0
Other	5.3	5.6	50.4	49.6
Manufacturing				
Sewing/tailoring	1.7	2.0	47.4	52.6
Arts and crafts	0.7	0.4	66.6	33.4
Shoe repair	0.5	0.5	50.0	50.0
Furniture making	0.4	0.6	40.0	60.0
Security (gates and burglar bars)	0.1	0.4	20.0	80.0
Waste recycling	0.0	0.1	0.0	100.0
Other	0.6	1.9	24.0	76.0

Note: Multiple response question

Table 8 shows that at least some South Africans and refugees are involved in every activity. However, the two groups also tend to occupy and dominate different market niches. South Africans are more strongly represented in food retail (the main exception being confectionary and the sale of canned drinks with roughly equal participation). Around 70% of the entrepreneurs who were selling fresh produce and cooked food were South Africans. On the other hand, over 70% of those selling most types of personal and household products were refugees. In the service sector, refugees dominate haircutting and braiding, as well as car repairs and IT. South Africans tend to dominate shoe repairs, transportation and car washing and guarding. There is less differentiation in the manufacturing sector, although the overall number of participants is small compared with retail and services.

Fourth, there was a significant difference in the amount of start-capital used by the two groups (Figure 2). Almost 80% of the South Africans started their businesses with less than ZAR5,000, while the equivalent figure was only 27% for refugees. At the other end of the spectrum, only 6% of the South Africans had start-up capital of more than ZAR20,000 compared to 43% of the refugees. This certainly suggests that refugees have access to greater amounts of start-up capital but it may also be that the barriers to entry are much lower in the food sector (which is dominated by South Africans) as the initial spend on stock is likely to be much lower than for businesses selling personal and household goods. It is significant that of the 28% of refugees who started with less than ZAR5,000, most were food retailers.

FIGURE 2: Amount of Start-Up Capital

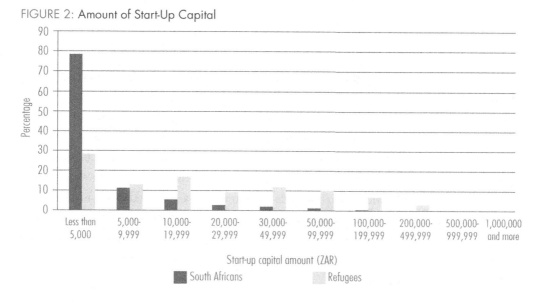

Fifth, both groups had added value to their businesses since start-up (Table 9). For example, while 78% of South Africans started with less than ZAR5,000, only 40% valued their enterprise as still less than ZAR5,000 (a fall of 38%). Similarly, with refugees the equivalent figures were 28% and 9% (a fall of 19%). The proportion of South African businesses with a current value of over ZAR20,000 was 25% (compared to only 6% at start-up). In the case of refugees, the equivalent figures were 70% and 43%. In other words, 19% of South Africans and 27% of refugees had moved into the highest value bracket.

TABLE 9: Current Business Value

	South Africans		Refugees	
	No.	%	No.	%
Less than ZAR5,000	349	40.1	75	8.5
ZAR5,000-9,999	177	20.3	83	9.4
ZAR10,000-19,999	128	14.7	110	12.4
ZAR20,000-29,999	57	6.6	110	12.4
ZAR30,000-49,999	59	6.8	115	13.0
ZAR50,000-99,999	46	5.3	148	16.7
ZAR100,000-199,999	28	3.2	135	15.2
ZAR200,000-499,999	18	2.1	93	10.5
ZAR500,000-999,999	3	0.3	12	1.4
<=ZAR1,000,000	5	0.6	5	0.6
Total	870	100.0	886	100.0

To assess the statistical significance of these differences, key variable comparisons were drawn out from the frequency distributions and binned into binary-level variables. These included (a) year of establishment (<=2010 and >2010); (b) start-up capital (<ZAR5,000 and >ZAR5,000); and (c) current business value (<ZAR5,000 and >ZAR5,000). The odds ratio calculations performed in Table 10 provide convergent validity for the observed frequency distributions. Independent of the influence of any other variables, the South African entrepreneurs had almost twice the odds of running a business established before 2011, almost 10 times the odds of starting a business with less than ZAR5,000 and almost seven times the odds of running a business currently valued at less than ZAR5,000. All of these comparisons yielded p-values less than the alpha of 0.01 on both the Pearson's chi-square test and the Fisher's exact test.

TABLE 10: Odds Ratio Calculations of Business Characteristics

Variables	Odds ratio	95% C.I.		P-values	
		Lower	Upper	Chi-square	Fisher's exact test
Established business before 2011**	1.993	1.67	2.379	<.001	<.001
Less than ZAR5,000 in start-up amount**	9.579	7.772	11.807	<.001	<.001
Less than ZAR5,000 in current value **	7.243	5.515	9.514	<.001	<.001
* p<.05 on both Pearson's chi-square and Fisher's exact test					
** p<.01 on both Pearson's chi-square and Fisher's exact test					
Note: Odds ratios measure change in odds from refugee to South African entrepreneurs					

BUSINESS STRATEGIES

Given the official and business literature perception that non-South Africans are much better at running businesses than their South African counterparts, it is important to find out whether the two groups pursue different business strategies and activities. The first point of comparison concerns where the two groups choose to locate their business operations. In the case of Cape Town, there are areas of the city where each group tends to dominate: refugee businesses are more common in the CBD and Bellville, for instance, while South Africans are more commonly located along transport routes in and out of the city, such as on streets and at taxi ranks and bus terminals. This difference is clear from Table 11. Half of the South Africans operate stalls on roadsides and 21% at taxi ranks. This compares with only 31% and 2% of refugees respectively. The other major difference is that half of the refugees operate from a fixed shop or workshop, compared to only 8% of the South Africans.

In addition to the observed variations in business location, the reasons for locational decisions also varied between the two groups (Table 12). When compared with the refugees, the South African migrant entrepreneurs had higher odds of choosing a business location based on it having the greatest number of customers, the tradition of doing business in a location, the cheapness of land, and the limited number of police in the area. The refugees had higher odds of choosing their business location based on other locational factors, especially access to services, property rentals, safety concerns, and distance from competitors.

TABLE 11: Usual Location of Business Activities

Business location	South Africans		Refugees	
	No.	%	No.	%
Temporary stall on the street/roadside	290	27.2	166	16.5
Permanent stall on the street/roadside	246	23.0	147	14.6
Taxi rank	221	20.7	22	2.2
In my home	102	9.6	34	3.4
No fixed location, mobile	87	8.1	26	2.6
Workshop or shop	86	8.1	525	52.1
Permanent stall in a market	87	8.1	106	10.5
Bus terminal	52	4.9	9	0.9
Railway station	21	2.0	1	0.1
Vehicle (car, truck, motor bike, bike)	19	1.8	3	0.3
In customer's home	16	1.5	16	1.6
Craft market	6	0.6	7	0.7
Restaurant or hotel	2	0.2	8	0.8
Other	37	3.5	38	3.8

Note: Multiple response question

TABLE 12: Odds Ratio Calculations of Reasons for Business Location

Reasons	Odds ratio	95% C.I. for O.R.		P-values	
		Lower	Upper	Chi-square	Fisher's exact test
Place with greatest number of customers**	2.231	1.707	2.915	<.001	<.001
Access to services such as water/electricity**	0.341	0.284	0.409	<.001	<.001
Have a permit to operate there**	0.746	0.624	0.893	.001	.001
Rents are cheaper	0.969	0.807	1.163	0.732	0.744
Safer than other locations**	0.673	0.564	0.803	<.001	<.001
Due to passing traffic	0.949	0.775	1.163	0.615	0.641
Close to home	0.869	0.73	1.036	0.117	0.118
Own/rent the land**	0.458	0.381	0.55	<.001	<.001
Close to other enterprises*	0.825	0.692	0.984	0.032	0.035
Distant from other competitors**	0.647	0.534	0.784	<.001	<.001

Always done business there**	1.262	1.061	1.501	0.009	0.009
Close to public transport	0.987	0.811	1.2	0.893	0.92
Cheap land**	1.739	1.424	2.123	<.001	<.001
Few or no police*	1.251	1.017	1.54	0.034	0.035

* p<.05 on both Pearson's chi-square and Fisher's exact test

** p<.01 on both Pearson's chi-square and Fisher's exact test

Note: Odds ratios measure change in odds from refugee to South African entrepreneurs

Refugee entrepreneurs were much more likely than South Africans to rent their business premises (Table 13). Almost 60% paid rent to a South African landlord. Another 13% paid rent to the municipality (as did 10% of the South Africans). Nearly 50% of South Africans operated their businesses rent free, compared to only 5% of refugees. What this means, in effect, is that around three-quarters of South Africans do not pay any rent for their premises, while over 80% of refugees do. The refugee entrepreneurs also pay a higher monthly rent, on average, than those South Africans who do pay rent (ZAR4,000 per month versus ZAR2,820 per month). In effect, many South Africans are able to augment their household income through renting business premises to refugees and therefore benefit from their presence.

TABLE 13: Occupancy/Tenure Status of Business Premises

Tenure status	South Africans		Refugees	
	No.	%	No.	%
Rent-free, with permission	276	26.1	58	5.8
I own it/am part owner	256	24.2	48	4.8
Rent-free, without permission (squatting)	214	20.3	59	5.9
Pay rent to private owner who is a South African (company or individual)	145	13.7	595	59.7
Pay rent to council/municipality	104	9.8	126	12.7
Share space/premises with others	28	2.7	2	0.2
Pay rent to private owner who is not a South African (company or individual)	17	1.6	91	9.1
Other	16	1.5	17	1.7

Another area of business strategy comparison concerns where the two groups source their goods and whether they tend to patronize the same outlets (Table 14). Most of the respondent refugees buy their supplies at wholesalers while South Africans patronize wholesalers and supermarkets in almost equal numbers. South African respondents also obtain goods from fresh produce markets and directly from farms in greater numbers. With the exception of factory purchase, refugees tend to spend more on average at all outlets. For example, while fewer refugees patronize supermarkets, their average monthly spend is ZAR8,693 compared with only ZAR3,219 by the South Africans. In total, the South African respondents spend more than the refugees at supermarkets, at fresh produce markets and directly from farms. Refugees spend five times as much on average at wholesalers and far more in total (ZAR21 million compared to less than ZAR2 million).

TABLE 14: Patronage of Different Suppliers

Source	South Africans			Refugees		
	% using source	Mean monthly spend (ZAR)	Total annual spend (ZAR)	% using source	Mean monthly spend (ZAR)	Total annual spend (ZAR)
Wholesaler	27.8	6,248	1,855,724	61.0	34,728	21,357,827
Supermarkets	27.3	3,219	936,642	8.5	8,693	747,640
Small shops/retailers	11.4	1,798	219,407	11.0	6,282	697,350
Fresh produce markets	9.6	4,751	489,364	4.9	16,869	826,600
Direct from farms	9.6	8,875	905,270	1.2	14,708	176,500
Direct from factory	7.4	32,216	2,545,050	8.2	11,924	977,800
South African informal sector enterprises	5.5	1,956	115,391	3.2	5,391	172,520
Non-South African informal sector enterprises	3.2	1,607	54,650	6.7	13,246	887,500
Other sources	5.1	3,486	188,250	4.6	10,838	498,525

There is a common assumption that other strategies adopted by refugees give them a strong competitive advantage over South Africans. In addition to greater business acumen and skills, they have been viewed, inter alia, as securing discounts through group purchasing, offering credit to consumers, operating for longer hours, and selling goods more cheaply. Statistical comparison of these, and other, business strategies indicates their relative importance to each group (Table 15). The refugees had lower odds of adjusting their operating hours to times of the day when there were most customers, and purchasing insurance. South African migrant entrepreneurs had lower odds of operating for extended hours (0.743) and individual bulk purchasing (0.67). Also, the refugees had two to three times the odds of keeping business records (0.475), selling goods more cheaply than competitors (0.395), purchasing in bulk with others (0.244), and negotiating with suppliers (0.340).

TABLE 15: Odds Ratio Calculations of Business Strategies

	Odds ratio	95% C.I. for O.R.		P-values	
		Lower	Upper	Chi-square	Fisher's exact test
I open my business only during the periods of the day when I have the most customers*	1.213	1.020	1.443	0.029	0.030
I purchase insurance	1.078	0.732	1.587	0.703	0.768
I offer credit to customers	0.918	0.770	1.093	0.336	0.348
I extend my hours of operation**	0.743	0.620	0.890	0.001	0.001
I purchase stock in bulk myself**	0.670	0.562	0.800	<.001	<.001
I charge different prices for different customers**	0.660	0.545	0.799	<.001	<.001
I look for the cheapest prices for goods by consulting the media**	0.656	0.538	0.800	<.001	<.001
I engage in shareholding**	0.562	0.437	0.722	<.001	<.001
I keep records of my business accounts**	0.475	0.398	0.566	<.001	<.001
I look for the cheapest prices for goods by asking other entrepreneurs**	0.439	0.367	0.525	<.001	<.001
I sell goods more cheaply than my competitors**	0.395	0.325	0.481	<.001	<.001
I purchase stock in bulk together with others**	0.344	0.278	0.424	<.001	<.001
I negotiate prices with my suppliers**	0.340	0.284	0.407	<.001	<.001
I look for cheapest prices for goods by calling suppliers**	0.230	0.191	0.278	<.001	<.001
* p<.05 on both Pearson's chi-square and Fisher's exact test					
** p<.01 on both Pearson's chi-square and Fisher's exact test					
Note: Odds ratios measure change in odds from refugee to South African entrepreneurs					

The final point of business strategy comparison concerns the hiring practices of the two groups of entrepreneurs. Almost half of the refugee entrepreneurs have employees compared to only 21% of the South Africans. The refugees in this sample provided three times as many jobs as the South Africans. Table 16 provides statistical confirmation of the greater employment-generating potential of refugees using odds ratio, chi-square and Fisher's exact test calculations.

TABLE 16: Odds Ratio Calculations for Employment-Generation

Variables	Odds ratio	95% C.I.		P-values	
		Lower	Upper	Chi-square	Fisher's exact test
Currently have employees**	0.273	0.225	0.332	<.001	<.001
* p<.05 on both Pearson's chi-square and Fisher's exact test					
** p<.01 on both Pearson's chi-square and Fisher's exact test					
Note: Odds ratios measure change in odds from refugee to South African entrepreneurs					

A breakdown of employees by sex and national origin shows some differences in the hiring patterns of the two groups (Table 17). In total, 9% of refugees hire South African men full-time and 1% part-time. The equivalent figures for South African enterprises are 8% and 4%. Refugees show a preference for hiring South African women over men with 16% employing women full-time and 4% part-time (compared to 9% and 1% for men). In the sample as a whole, 30% are South Africans employed by refugees and 28% are South Africans employed by other South Africans. This suggests that both refugee and South African enterprises create jobs for South Africans in roughly equal numbers. The major difference is in the employment of non-South Africans. Less than 5% of the total number of employees are non-South Africans employed by South Africans, whereas 39% are non-South Africans employed by refugees.

TABLE 17: Employment Categories of Informal Business Employees

Employee categories	South Africans			Refugees		
	Total no. of employees	% of total entrepre-neurs	% of all employees	Total no. of employees	% of total entrepre-neurs	% of all employees
South African males (full-time)	166	8.0	10.8	145	9.1	9.5
South African females (full-time)	172	8.0	11.2	231	15.9	15.1
South African males (part-time)	66	3.6	4.3	16	1.1	1.0
South African females (part-time)	29	1.8	1.9	61	4.1	4.0
Non-South African males (full/part-time)	27	1.7	1.8	406	21.8	26.5
Non-South African females (full/part-time)	21	1.7	1.8	194	11.9	12.6

COMPARATIVE SECURITY RISKS

Table 18 presents the aggregated results of the security risks question for the two groups of entrepreneurs. First, it is clear from the table that not every South African and refugee respondent has been affected. This is an important initial finding because it does suggest that most informal entrepreneurs are able to run their businesses without significant inter-ference. This may be because of where they are located or the measures and precautions they take to protect themselves. Second, it is clear that South Africans are not immune from any of these risks. Nearly a third had been robbed of their stock and nearly 20% had had income stolen. The degree of vulnerability to other security risks was much lower but not non-existent. To this extent, therefore, South Africans in the informal sector are also victims of crime. But there is no support here for the contention that South Africans and non-South Africans are equally at risk or victimized.

TABLE 18: Security Risks Facing Refugee and South African Entrepreneurs

	Refugees % affected	South Africans % affected
Prejudice against my nationality	48.0	2.2
Crime/theft of goods/stock	47.8	30.9
Crime/theft of money/income	38.1	18.5
Verbal insults against my business	34.2	7.9
Conflict with South African entrepreneurs	32.7	21.1
Conflict with refugee entrepreneurs	27.1	19.0
Physical attacks/assaults by South Africans	21.4	3.5
Harassment/demand of bribes by police	18.7	5.5
Confiscation of goods by police	14.7	6.4
Arrest/detention of entrepreneur/employees	8.5	1.4
Physical attacks/assaults by police	7.9	1.1
Prejudice against my gender	6.5	5.0

On every count, the proportion of refugees affected was higher, sometimes significantly so. For example, 47% of refugees cited prejudice against their nationality as a risk to their business, compared to only 2% of South Africans. Also, 34% of refugees were affected by verbal insults against their business, compared to only 8% of South Africans. Forty-eight percent of refugees, compared with 31% of South Africans, had been affected by theft of their goods and stock. Similarly, 38% of refugees, compared with 19% of South Africans, had been affected by theft of their income. Refugees reported higher levels of conflict with South African competitors (33%) than South Africans did with refugees (19%) and with other South Africans (21%). Interestingly, refugees also reported higher levels of conflict with other refugee businesses (27%). The details and outcomes of such conflicts need further research, but the findings suggest that we cannot assume that refugees are a homogenous group with identical interests.

The descriptive comparisons which suggest that refugees are more likely than South Africans to be affected by the various security risks are validated statistically in Table 19. South African entrepreneurs had lower odds of experiencing all potential risks on the list. Refugees were nearly three times more likely to be victims of theft of income and five times more likely to be subject to demands for bribes by police. The odds of a refugee entrepreneur being physically assaulted, experiencing prejudice, and being arrested and detained were over five times higher than for South Africans.

TABLE 19: Odds Ratio Calculations for Business Problems

	Odds ratio	95% confidence interval		Pearson chi-square	Df	P-value 2-sided	n
		Lower	Upper				
Prejudice against my gender	0.782	0.539	1.136	1.671	1	0.196	2051
Conflict with refugee entrepreneurs**	0.644	0.524	0.792	17.489	1	<.001	2056
Conflict with South African entrepreneurs**	0.552	0.453	0.673	34.938	1	<.001	2054
Crime/theft of goods/stock**	0.492	0.411	0.589	60.363	1	<.001	2052
Crime/theft of money/income**	0.373	0.305	0.456	95.509	1	<.001	2050
Harassment/demands for bribes by police**	0.241	0.176	0.330	88.722	1	<.001	2046
Confiscation of goods by police**	0.403	0.298	0.545	36.629	1	<.001	2047
Arrest/detention of yourself/employees**	0.179	0.105	0.303	50.513	1	<.001	2045
Verbal insults against your business**	0.167	0.129	0.216	214.406	1	<.001	2050
Physical attacks/assaults by police**	0.158	0.089	0.282	50.517	1	<.001	2052
Physical attacks/assaults by other South Africans**	0.137	0.096	0.196	150.979	1	<.001	2047
Prejudice against my nationality**	0.025	0.017	0.039	577.723	1	<.001	2049

*p<.05

**p<.01

Note: Odds ratios measure change in odds from refugee to South African entrepreneurs

In theory, we might expect to see higher degrees of informal business security risks for both groups in large cities such as Cape Town compared to the much smaller towns of Limpopo (Table 20). In the case of refugees, and with the exceptions of prejudice, verbal insults and treatment by police, Limpopo was indeed safer than Cape Town. For South Africans, Cape Town was also a more dangerous place to run a business. For example, 56% of refugees and 31% of South Africans had experienced theft of goods in Cape Town. In Limpopo, the equivalent figures were 38% and 30%, a much lower spread than in Cape Town. In both locations, however, the risks are significantly higher for refugees than South

Africans. Indeed, refugees in Limpopo were less secure than South Africans in both Limpopo and Cape Town. Theft of goods had affected 38% of refugees in Limpopo compared with around 30% of South Africans in both Limpopo and Cape Town. Also, 31% of refugees in Limpopo had experienced theft of money compared with 12% of South Africans in Limpopo and 26% in Cape Town. Some 19% of Limpopo refugees had experienced physical assaults or attacks compared with 2% of South Africans in Limpopo and 7% in Cape Town.

TABLE 20: Security Risks Facing Refugee and South African Entrepreneurs by Location

	Cape Town		Limpopo	
	Refugees % affected	South Africans % affected	Refugees % affected	South Africans % affected
Prejudice against my nationality	47.2	3.6	47.6	1.1
Crime/theft of goods/stock	56.2	30.9	38.3	30.4
Crime/theft of money/income	43.8	25.7	31.3	11.8
Verbal insults against my business	32.1	9.0	35.3	6.9
Conflict with South African entrepreneurs	34.5	20.3	30.2	21.4
Conflict with refugee entrepreneurs	27.9	15.7	25.6	22.1
Physical attacks/assaults by South Africans	23.0	5.8	19.0	1.6
Harassment/demand of bribes by police	10.5	6.6	26.2	3.9
Confiscation of goods by police	10.1	8.0	18.8	4.9
Arrest/detention of entrepreneur/employees	7.5	2.0	9.1	1.2
Physical attacks/assaults by police	6.7	1.6	8.7	1.1
Prejudice against my gender	5.8	6.8	6.9	3.5

Another common belief is that security risks are higher in informal settlements than in other parts of the city, particularly as many of the reports of violence against businesses come from informal settlements, which also have much higher general crime levels. To test this hypothesis, we focused only on Cape Town and divided refugees and South Africans into two groups according to whether they were operating in an informal or formal part of the city (Table 21). For both refugees and South Africans, the risks are higher in informal settlements across almost all indicators. However, the difference in the degree of risk between refugees and South Africans is significantly greater in informal settlements than it is in formal areas of the city. The only indicator where formal areas are riskier for both is in the chances of having goods confiscated by the police. Since the police barely venture into large swathes of informal settlement, this is not surprising. Refugees are slightly more likely to experience theft of goods in the formal versus informal areas (57% versus 54%) but the difference is small and indicates that this is a major risk for most businesses irrespective of location.

TABLE 21: Security Risks Facing Refugee and South African Entrepreneurs in Cape Town

	Formal areas		Informal areas	
	Refugees % affected	South Africans % affected	Refugees % affected	South Africans % affected
Prejudice against my nationality	44.9	1.7	53.8	6.2
Crime/theft of goods/stock	57.0	26.7	53.8	36.7
Crime/theft of money/income	41.4	19.5	50.8	34.3
Verbal insults against my business	30.1	6.8	37.9	11.9
Conflict with South African entrepreneurs	29.6	20.9	48.5	19.5
Conflict with refugee entrepreneurs	25.5	18.5	34.8	11.9
Physical attacks/assaults by South Africans	21.2	3.8	28.0	8.6
Harassment/demand for bribes by police	8.9	8.6	15.2	3.8
Confiscation of goods by police	10.2	8.9	9.8	6.7
Arrest/detention of entrepreneur and/or employees	5.1	1.7	14.4	2.4
Physical attacks/assaults by police	4.8	0.7	12.1	2.9
Prejudice against my gender	5.6	4.1	6.1	10.5

Unsurprisingly, refugees were far more likely than South Africans to say that their business operations had been negatively affected by xenophobia: 38% versus 5% (Table 22). There are two possible reasons for South Africans being affected: first, when collective violence occurs at a particular localized settlement, it is possible that in the chaos and mayhem, South African-owned businesses may be caught up in the looting and vandalism. As one South African owner noted, "when these attacks start, it becomes difficult for us to move and every business becomes a target. Xenophobia does not only affect foreigners, it affects everyone" (Interview, 3 March 2016). A second explanation is that there are cascading, spillover effects on those South African small businesses with cooperative, dependent relationships and linkages with affected migrant-operated businesses.

TABLE 22: Degree of Impact of Xenophobia on Business Operations

	Refugees %	South Africans %
A great deal	18.3	1.4
To some extent	19.3	3.5
Not very much	18.4	5.7
Not at all	43.9	89.4

STRATEGIES OF SELF-PROTECTION

The dangerous and unpredictable environment in which informal entrepreneurs ply their trade in South African cities presents serious security challenges. It is clear from the previous section that while both groups are affected, refugees are at much greater risk than South Africans to a range of threats. There is no a priori reason why this might be the case, other than the fact that refugees are targeted because their presence is viewed by citizens and officials as unwelcome and even illegitimate. This was certainly the view of most of the refugees interviewed for this study who consistently identified the manifestations of xenophobia as the major security problem they faced:

> We are victims of verbal attacks by clients. They say things such as "you must go to [your] country. Mandela is already dead. What are you doing here?" (Interview with Congolese refugee, 25 February 2016).

> Some [customers] swear at me, my customers sometimes steal from me and when you catch them, they tell you harshly that you are a foreigner. And that you need to go back to your country. You are always faced with difficulties when you are a foreigner and as such you need to be patient and know how to deal with different kinds of people. There is too much disrespect here from South Africans because even someone who is way younger than you, they can swear and say nasty things to you if you are a foreigner. And they tell you straight that South Africa is their country (Interview with Somali refugee, 12 March 2016).

If you are a foreigner, you are always affected by xenophobia. There is no way that you can live here and not be affected. Xenophobia starts from your customer. Some customers are very rude and if you respond, they will talk to you in their own language and scold you and then tell you to go back [to your country]. They have bad words for foreigners. Many times, my business was robbed when I was in Johannesburg. It was because I was a foreigner because they rarely stole from locals. Sometimes criminals would come to you and ask you to give them money and they would just ask you the foreigner. Why not the local people? That is xenophobia (Interview with Ethiopian refugee, 19 March 2016).

Xenophobia affects us all. We know who we are. We are foreigners and that doesn't change. Nothing changes the reality. We live under alert anytime, no matter the set up in which we are operating in. We always know that the same people we are dealing with can anytime become a danger to us. It is difficult to trust any person in South Africa. The person who is with you here today, when there is a protest and foreigners are being attacked, he will be the first to attack you. There is no safety. I have not been attacked but I have seen other people being attacked and it is serious. It kills your business and it can also kill you (Interview with Congolese refugee, 25 February 2016).

Xenophobia is the most critical problem. I have been directly affected and have been caught up in the troubles. People have harassed me a lot, just talking like they want to kill you or to burn you or other such things. But that was when I was in Durban. Here [Cape Town] I have not been harassed. But there are many people who have been victims. They have been harassed and their goods destroyed, especially when there are strikes. The people just target anything that they can get. They are very cruel and they do not care what the owner will do to survive (Interview with Congolese refugee, 19 February 2016).

Xenophobia affects everyone who is a foreigner. When people loot your shop is that not xenophobia? When they chase you away from operating in an area because you are a foreigner that is xenophobia. There is xenophobia here, everywhere in this country. I have friends in other parts of the country, it is xenophobia where they live. I think South Africa is the only country with such xenophobia. I have been affected many times. When I was in Gugulethu, we were robbed. That was xenophobia because they were robbing foreign-owned shops. Here I have been affected once during a strike and they took some things from the shop. So, xenophobia is everywhere here. The community leaders do not protect us during the strikes. Some of the leaders are at the forefront of looting when strikes occur, so how can they help? The government must protect us from xenophobia and crime. The police need to do their work better because right now they are not (Interview with Somali refugee, 7 March 2016).

Inadequate police protection and failure to respond when refugee businesses are under attack deepens exposure to security risks. A Congolese refugee said that the only recourse available was to "run away" as the "police here in such instances, they don't protect us, but instead abuse us" (Interview, Cape Town, 5 March 2016). Others displayed similar distrust of the police because of perceptions of bias:

The police are not very helpful. If you have a case against a South African, they will always side with the South African. So, it's a waste of time to report a case against a South African (Interview with Congolese refugee, 24 February 2016).

How accurate are these perceptions of South African hostility towards refugee businesses and business owners? A 2010 SAMP national survey of South African citizens found that only 20% were in favour of making it easier for migrants to establish small businesses and for migrant traders to buy and sell.[27] Only 25% felt that refugees should be allowed to work in South Africa. A similar proportion said that they would take part in actions to prevent migrants operating a business in their neighbourhood, 15% that they would combine with others to force migrants to leave, and 11% that they were prepared to use violence against them. Over 55% agreed with the proposition that migrants were victims of violence because they did not belong in South Africa. Only 36% said that refugees should always enjoy police protection and 25% that they should never enjoy protection.

A number of studies have suggested that to lower the risks of victimization, migrants should adopt various measures to protect themselves and their employees.[28] This survey sought to establish how common some of these strategies are and whether they are also adopted by South Africans (Table 23). One of the most common strategies is risk-sharing by partnering with other businesses. Nearly a third of refugees and 17% of South Africans adopt risk-sharing through partnership. Staying overnight on business premises (often a modified container) is a strategy pursued by both groups but, again, by more refugees (19% versus 9% of South Africans). There have been several high profile shootings of robbers by refugees under attack but this survey found that only 6% keep weapons for self-protection. Other strategies (pursued by less than 10% of refugees and 5% of South Africans) include paying security guards, and paying protection money to the police or community leaders. Around 5% of both groups purchase insurance. Table 24 analyzes if the differences between the refugees and South Africans are statistically significant. With the exception of paying for insurance, refugees were far more likely than South Africans to adopt strategies of self-protection. Refugees were five times as likely to pay for protection and twice as likely to sleep on their business premises and to partner with others to distribute risk.

TABLE 23: Self-Protection Strategies Used by Informal Sector Entrepreneurs

	Refugees %	South Africans %
I partner with other businesses to distribute risks	31.0	17.4
I sleep on my business premises	18.8	8.7
I pay for security guards	7.3	1.9
I keep weapons for self-protection	5.8	4.0
I pay the police for protection	5.5	1.0
I purchase insurance	5.1	5.5
I pay community leaders for protection	2.5	0.6

TABLE 24: Odds Ratio Calculations of Business Strategies

	Odds ratio	95% C.I. for O.R.		P-Values	
		Lower	Upper	Chi-square	Fisher's exact test
I purchase insurance	1.078	0.732	1.587	0.703	0.768
I keep weapons for self-protection*	0.648	0.430	0.976	0.037	0.039
I partner with other businesses to distribute risks**	0.470	0.382	0.579	<.001	<.001
I sleep in my business premises**	0.411	0.315	0.537	<.001	<.001
I pay for security guards**	0.245	0.148	0.405	<.001	<.001
I pay community leaders for protection**	0.222	0.091	0.543	<.001	<.001
I pay the police for protection**	0.180	0.094	0.347	<.001	<.001
*p<.05 on both Pearson's chi-square and Fisher's exact test					
**p<.01 on both Pearson's chi-square and Fisher's exact test					
Note: Odds ratios measure change in odds from refugee to South African entrepreneurs					

Various other strategies emerged during the in-depth interviews although it is not known how common these are. For example, some refugees said that they hire South Africans to assist in communication with customers and also because it reduces their vulnerability to violence. In addition to paying protection money to police and community leaders, refugees in one part of Cape Town regularly pay protection money to the local taxi association. The taxi association then uses this to extort money from South Africans in the area too. Others make sure that they do not keep all their stock on the business premises out of fear that they will be cleaned out during looting or confiscation of goods by the police. Still others open for business only when they know that the police are not patrolling.

CONCLUSION

This report set out to systematically compare the informal enterprises established by different categories of migrant in South African urban areas. This comparative analysis of refugees and internal migrants suggests that there is a need for much greater nuance in policy and academic discussions about the impact of refugee migration on the South African informal economy. The stereotyping of refugees in public discourse as undermining and destroying South African competitors is clearly far removed from the reality. While refugees seem able to access greater amounts of start-up capital (although neither they nor South Africans can access formal bank loans), both groups seem able to grow their businesses. Partly this is because they tend to occupy different niches in the informal economy with South Africans focused more on the food sector and refugees on services and retailing household goods. This may help to explain another difference between the two with refugees tending to patronize wholesalers for their supplies and South Africans purchasing from supermarkets and fresh produce markets.

The idea promulgated by the Minister of Small Business Development that refugees have a competitive advantage with entrepreneurship "in their blood" is clearly fallacious. South Africa's refugee legislation and restrictive employment policies mean that working for, and then establishing, an informal enterprise is virtually the only available livelihood option. But to argue that all refugees come to South Africa with a pre-existing skill and business experience is misplaced. Instead, refugees (like small business owners everywhere) are extremely motivated, hard-working and dedicated. They employ several business strategies to achieve monetary success although business expansion is hampered by the fact that only a portion of profits can be reinvested in the business, with the rest used to support dependants in South Africa and their home country. These strategies are not illegal or even underhanded, but quite transparent and could be emulated. And to suggest, as the minister also did, that South African migrants are poor business people is just as fallacious. While it is true that the odds of refugees pursuing a particular strategy, such as giving goods on credit, are generally higher than South Africans doing so, this does not mean that no South Africans pursue the strategy, as many clearly do. Instead of constantly pitting refugees against South Africans as the official mind likes to do, it would be more productive to treat them in policy terms as a single group attempting, often against considerable odds, to establish and grow small businesses in a hostile or indifferent economic and political environment.

This report has also undertaken a comparative risks assessment and vulnerabilities analysis for refugee and South African entrepreneurs operating small business ventures in the informal economies of Cape Town and various towns of Limpopo province. The results show that while both groups are exposed to several risks concurrently, refugee enterprises are far more vulnerable and overexposed. The social and structural insecurity experienced by refugee entrepreneurs is unambiguous from several key findings. Despite operating in the same localized environment and under similar conditions, this group encounters a more challenging set of hurdles and on a more frequent basis. The general effect of operating small businesses in the informal economic sector does make business owners of all kinds vulnerable, but this alone cannot explain the greater vulnerabilities of the refugee cohort. Instead, xenophobia and their status as "outsiders" adds another layer of risks for such operators. Limited access to police protection and mistreatment by officers only exacerbates this insecurity.

What is also evident is that the majority of refugee operators have not, to date, been affected by a range of potential risks. In part, this may be because of the mitigation strategies that they adopt. As refugee and migrant communities grow in South Africa, the emergence of individuals who are able to mitigate common risks and build their enterprises successfully is to be expected. But rather than treating these achievements with suspicion and negativity, as government tends to do, greater attempts need to be made to harness these productive capacities for the growth of local informal, entrepreneurial economies. These successes are not an abnormal development nor particularly driven by unfair advantages or illicit practices. Ultimately, comprehensive national and localized strategies are required to develop and support informal entrepreneurship and small business growth in South Africa.

ENDNOTES

1   Zwane (2014).

2   Ibid.

3   Hutchinson and de Beer (2013); Iwu et al. (2016); Ligthelm (2011); Preisendörfer et al. (2012a, 2012b, 2014a, 2014b).

4   Charman et al. (2012).

5   Basardien et al. (2014: 57).

6   Basardien et al. (2014).

7   Choto et al. (2014); Iwu et al. (2016).

8   Radipere (2012); Radipere and Dhliwayo (2014).

9   Callaghan and Venter (2011).

10 Callaghan (2013).

11 Abor and Quartey (2010); Crush et al. (2015); Fatoki (2016); Fatoki and Patswawairi (2012); Grant (2013); Thompson (2016); Willemse (2011).

12 Callaghan and Venter (2011); Gastrow and Amit (2015); Ligthelm (2011); Rogerson (2016a, 2016b); Venter (2012).

13 Rogerson (2016a).

14 Rogerson (2016b); Skinner (2008).

15 Supreme Court (2014: 25).

16 Crush and Ramachandran (2015a).

17 Crush and Ramachandran (2014).

18 Charman and Piper (2012); Charman et al. (2012); Piper and Charman (2016).

19 Charman and Piper (2012: 81).

20 Charman and Piper (2012: 89).

21 Piper and Charman (2016: 332).

22 Williams and Gurtoo (2010).

23 Crea et al. (2016); Jinnah (2010); Kavuro (2015); Ragunanan and Smit (2011).

24 Graham and De Lannoy (2016); Klasen and Woolard (2009).

25 Williams (2007, 2015); Williams and Gurtoo (2010); Williams and Youseff (2014).

26 Callaghan and Venter (2011); Fatoki and Patswawairi (2012); Khosa and Kalitanyi (2015); Venter (2012).

27 Crush et al. (2013: 32-8).

28 Gastrow (2013); Hikam (2011); Gastrow and Amit (2015); Ncwadi and Hikam (2015); Smit and Rugunanan (2014).

REFERENCES

1. Abor, J. and Quartey, P. (2010). Issues in SME Development in Ghana and South Africa. *International Research Journal of Finance and Economics* 39: 218-228.

2. Basardien, F., Parker, H., Bayat, M., Friedrich, C. and Sulaiman, A. (2014). Entrepreneurial Orientation of Spaza Shop Entrepreneurs: Evidence from a Study of South African and Somali-Owned Spaza Shop Entrepreneurs in Khayelitsha. *Singaporean Journal of Business Economics and Management Studies* 2: 45-61.

3. Bekker, S. (2015). Violent Xenophobic Episodes in South Africa, 2008 and 2015. *African Human Mobility Review* 1: 229-252.

4. Callaghan, C. (2013). Individual Values and Economic Performance of Inner-City Street Traders. *Journal of Economics* 4: 145-156.

5. Callaghan, C. and Venter, R. (2011). An Investigation of the Entrepreneurial Orientation, Context and Entrepreneurial Performance of Inner-City Johannesburg Street Traders. *Southern African Business Review* 15: 28-48.

6. Charman, A. and Govender, T. (2016). The Relational Economy of Informality: Spatial Dimensions of Street Trading in Ivory Park, South Africa. *Urban Forum* 27: 311-328.

7. Charman, A. and Petersen, L. (2015). A Transnational Space of Business: The Informal Economy of Ivory Park, Johannesburg. In J. Crush, A. Chikanda and C. Skinner (eds.), *Mean Streets: Migration, Xenophobia and Informality in South Africa* (Ottawa: IDRC), pp. 78-99.

8. Charman, A. and Piper, L. (2012). Xenophobia, Criminality and Violent Entrepreneurship: Violence against Somali Shopkeepers in Delft South, Cape Town, South Africa. *South African Review of Sociology* 43: 81-105.

9. Charman, A., Petersen, L. and Piper, L. (2012). From Local Survivalism to Foreign Entrepreneurship: The Transformation of the Spaza Sector in Delft, Cape Town. *Transformation* 78: 47-73.

10. Choto, P., Tengeh, R. and Iwu, C. (2014). Daring to Survive or to Grow? The Growth Aspirations and Challenges of Survivalist Entrepreneurs in South Africa. *Environmental Economics* 5: 93-101.

11. Crea, T., Loughry, M., O'Halloran, C. and Flannery, G. (2016). Environmental Risk: Urban Refugees' Struggles to Build Livelihoods in South Africa. *International Social Work* 60: 667-682.

12. Crush, J. and Ramachandran, S. 2014. *Xenophobic Violence in South Africa: Denialism, Minimalism, Realism*. SAMP Migration Policy Series No. 66. Cape Town.

13. Crush, J. and Ramachandran, S. 2015a. Doing Business with Xenophobia. In J. Crush, A. Chikanda and C. Skinner (eds.), *Mean Streets: Migration, Xenophobia and Informality in South Africa* (Ottawa: IDRC), pp. 25-59.

14. Crush, J., Chikanda, A. and Skinner, C. (Eds.). (2015). *Mean Streets: Migration, Xenophobia and Informality in South Africa*. Ottawa: IDRC.

15. Crush, J., Ramachandran, S. and Pendleton, W. (2013). *Soft Targets: Xenophobia, Public Violence and Changing Attitudes to Migrants in South Africa after May 2008*. SAMP Migration Policy Series No. 64, Cape Town.

16. Fatoki, O. (2016). Problems Experienced by Immigrant Spaza Shop Owners in South Africa. *Journal of Economics* 7: 100-106.

17. Fatoki, O. and Patswawairi, T. (2012). The Motivations and Obstacles to Immigrant Entrepreneurship in South Africa. *Journal of Social Science* 32: 133-142.

18. Gastrow, V. (2013). Business Robbery, The Foreign Trader and the Small Shop: How Business Robberies Affect Somali Traders in the Western Cape. *SA Crime Quarterly* 43: 5-15.

19. Gastrow, V. and Amit, R. (2015). The Role of Migrant Traders in Local Economies: A Case Study of Somali Spaza Shops in Cape Town. In J. Crush, A. Chikanda and C. Skinner (eds.), *Mean Streets: Migration, Xenophobia and Informality in South Africa* (Ottawa: IDRC), pp.162-177.

20. Graham, L. and De Lannoy, A. (2016). Youth Unemployment: What Can We Do in the Short Run? At: http://www.econ3x3.org/article/youth-unemployment-what-can-we-do-short-run

21. Grant, R. (2013). Gendered Spaces of Informal Entrepreneurship in Soweto, South Africa. *Urban Geography* 34: 86-108.

22. Harber, A. (2011). Foreigners Can Have No More Than Two Shops. In A. Harber, *Diepsloot* (Johannesburg: Jonathan Ball), pp. 120-135.

23. Hikam, A. 2011. An Exploratory Study on the Somali Immigrants' Involvement in the Informal Economy of Nelson Mandela Bay. MA Thesis, Nelson Mandela Metropolitan University, Port Elizabeth.

24. Hutchinson, M. and de Beer, M. (2013). An Exploration of Factors that Limit the Long-Term Survival and Development of Micro and Survivalist Enterprises: Empirical Evidence from the Informal Economy in South Africa. *Mediterranean Journal of Social Sciences* 4: 237-245.

25. Iwu, C., Gwija, S., Tengeh, R., Cupido, C. and Mason, R. (2016). The Unique Role of the Survivalist Retail Entrepreneur in Job Creation and Poverty Reduction: Implications for Active Stakeholder Participation. *Acta Universitatis Danubius (Economica)* 12: 16-37.

26. Jinnah, Z. (2010). Making Home in a Hostile Land: Understanding Somali Identity, Integration, Livelihood and Risks in Johannesburg. *Journal of Sociology and Social Anthropology* 1: 91-99.

27. Jordaan, N. (2015). Operation Fiela 'Demoralizes and Dehumanizes' Migrants. *Sunday Times*. July 22.

28. Kavuro, C. (2015). Refugees and Asylum Seekers: Barriers to Accessing South Africa's Labour Market. *Law, Democracy and Development* 19: 232-260.

29. Khosa, R. and Kalitanyi, V. (2015). Migration Reasons, Traits and Entrepreneurial Motivation of African Immigrant Entrepreneurs: Towards an Entrepreneurial Migration Progression. *Journal of Enterprising Communities* 9: 132-155.

30. Klasen, S. and Woolard, I. (2009). Surviving Unemployment Without State Support: Unemployment and Household Formation in South Africa. *Journal of African Economies* 18: 1-51.

31. Ligthelm, A. (2011). Survival Analysis of Small Informal Businesses in South Africa, 2007–2010. *Eurasian Business Review* 1: 160-179.

32. Masinga, L. (2015). Stop Using the Word Xenophobia. *Independent Online* July 10.

33. Misago, J-P. (2016). Responding to Xenophobic Violence in Post-Apartheid South Africa: Barking up the Wrong Tree. *African Human Mobility Review* 2: 443-467.

34. Ncwadi, R. and Hikam, A. (2015). Trans-Border Migration of African Migrants into South Africa: A Case Study of Somalian Informal Traders in Motherwell Township, South Africa. *International Journal of Managerial Studies and Research* 3: 118-135.

35. Ntema, J. (2016). Informal Home-Based Entrepreneurs in South Africa: How Non-South Africans Outcompete South Africans. *Africa Insight* 46: 44-59.

36. Peberdy, S. (2017). *Competition or Cooperation? South African and Migrant Entrepreneurs in Johannesburg.* SAMP Migration Policy Series No. 75, Cape Town.

37. Piper, L. and Charman, A. (2016). Xenophobia, Price Competition and Violence in the Spaza Sector in South Africa. *African Human Mobility Review*, 2 332-361.

38. Preisendörfer, P., Bitz, A. and Bezuidenhout, F. (2012a). Business Start-Ups and Their Prospects of Success in South African Townships. *South African Review of Sociology* 43: 3-23.

39. Preisendörfer, P., Bitz, A. and Bezuidenhout, F. (2012b). In Search of Black Entrepreneurship: Why is There a Lack of Entrepreneurial Activity Among the Black Population in South Africa. *Journal of Developmental Entrepreneurship* 17: 1-18.

40. Preisendörfer, P., Perks, S. and Bezuidenhout, F. (2014a). Do South African Townships Lack Entrepreneurial Spirit? *International Journal of Entrepreneurship and Small Business* 22: 159-178.

41. Preisendörfer, P., Bitz, A. and Bezuidenhout, F. (2014b). Black Entrepreneurship: A Case Study on Entrepreneurial Activities and Ambitions in a South African Township. *Journal of Enterprising Communities* 8: 162-179.

42. Radipere, N. (2012). An Analysis of Local and Immigrant Entrepreneurship in the South African Small Enterprise Sector (Gauteng Province). PhD Thesis, University of South Africa, Pretoria.

43. Radipere, S., and Dhliwayo, S. (2014). An Analysis of Local and Immigrant Entrepreneurs in South Africa's SME Sector. *Mediterranean Journal of Social Sciences* 5: 189-198.

44. Rugunanan P. and Smit, R. (2011). Seeking Refuge in South Africa: Challenges Facing a Group of Congolese and Burundian Refugees. *Development Southern Africa* 28: 705-718.

45. Rogerson, C. (2016a). Progressive Rhetoric, Ambiguous Policy Pathways: Street Trading in Inner-City Johannesburg, South Africa. *Local Economy* 31: 204-218.

46. Rogerson, C. (2016b). South Africa's Informal Economy: Reframing Debates in National Policy. *Local Economy* 31: 172-86.

47. Skinner, C. (2008). The Struggle for the Streets: Processes of Exclusion and Inclusion of Street Traders in Durban, South Africa. *Development Southern Africa* 25: 227-242.

48. Smit, R. and Rugunanan, P. (2014). From Precarious Lives to Precarious Work: The Dilemma Facing Refugees in Gauteng, South Africa. *South African Review of Sociology* 45: 4-26.

49. Supreme Court (2014). *Somali Association of South Africa v Limpopo Department of Economic Development, Environment and Tourism (48/2014)*. ZASCA 143 (September 26, 2014).

50. Thompson, D. (2016). Risky Business and Geography of Refugee Capitalism in the Somali Migrant Economy of Gauteng, South Africa. *Journal of Ethnic and Migration Studies* 42: 120-35.

51. Venter, R. (2012). Entrepreneurial Values, Hybridity and Entrepreneurial Capital: Insights from Johannesburg's Informal Sector. *Development Southern Africa* 29: 225-239.

52. Willemse, L. (2011). Opportunities and Constraints Facing Informal Traders: Evidence from Four South African Cities. *Town and Regional Planning* 59: 8-16.

53. Williams, C. (2007). Entrepreneurs Operating in the Informal Economy: Necessity or Opportunity Driven? *Journal of Small Business and Entrepreneurship* 20: 309-320.

54. Williams, C. (2015). Explaining the Informal Economy: An Exploratory Evaluation of Competing Perspectives. *Industrial Relations* 70: 741-765.

55. Williams, C. and Gurtoo, A. (2010). Evaluating Competing Theories of Street Entrepreneurship: Some Lessons from a Study of Street Vendors in Bangalore, India. *International Entrepreneurship and Management Journal* 8: 391-409.

56. Williams, C. and Youssef, Y. (2014). Is Informal Sector Entrepreneurship Necessity- or Opportunity-Driven? Some Lessons from Urban Brazil. *Business and Management Research* 3: 41-53.

57. Zwane, T. (2014). Spazas: Talking Shop is Good for Business. *Mail and Guardian*, November 6.

MIGRATION POLICY SERIES

1   *Covert Operations: Clandestine Migration, Temporary Work and Immigration Policy in South Africa* (1997) ISBN 1-874864-51-9

2   *Riding the Tiger: Lesotho Miners and Permanent Residence in South Africa* (1997) ISBN 1-874864-52-7

3   *International Migration, Immigrant Entrepreneurs and South Africa's Small Enterprise Economy* (1997) ISBN 1-874864-62-4

4   *Silenced by Nation Building: African Immigrants and Language Policy in the New South Africa* (1998) ISBN 1-874864-64-0

5   *Left Out in the Cold? Housing and Immigration in the New South Africa* (1998) ISBN 1-874864-68-3

6   *Trading Places: Cross-Border Traders and the South African Informal Sector* (1998) ISBN 1-874864-71-3

7   *Challenging Xenophobia: Myth and Realities about Cross-Border Migration in Southern Africa* (1998) ISBN 1-874864-70-5

8   *Sons of Mozambique: Mozambican Miners and Post-Apartheid South Africa* (1998) ISBN 1-874864-78-0

9   *Women on the Move: Gender and Cross-Border Migration to South Africa* (1998) ISBN 1-874864-82-9

10 *Namibians on South Africa: Attitudes Towards Cross-Border Migration and Immigration Policy* (1998) ISBN 1-874864-84-5

11 *Building Skills: Cross-Border Migrants and the South African Construction Industry* (1999) ISBN 1-874864-84-5

12 *Immigration & Education: International Students at South African Universities and Technikons* (1999) ISBN 1-874864-89-6

13 *The Lives and Times of African Immigrants in Post-Apartheid South Africa* (1999) ISBN 1-874864-91-8

14 *Still Waiting for the Barbarians: South African Attitudes to Immigrants and Immigration* (1999) ISBN 1-874864-91-8

15 *Undermining Labour: Migrancy and Sub-Contracting in the South African Gold Mining Industry* (1999) ISBN 1-874864-91-8

16 *Borderline Farming: Foreign Migrants in South African Commercial Agriculture* (2000) ISBN 1-874864-97-7

17 *Writing Xenophobia: Immigration and the Press in Post-Apartheid South Africa* (2000) ISBN 1-919798-01-3

18 *Losing Our Minds: Skills Migration and the South African Brain Drain* (2000) ISBN 1-919798-03-x

19 *Botswana: Migration Perspectives and Prospects* (2000) ISBN 1-919798-04-8

20 *The Brain Gain: Skilled Migrants and Immigration Policy in Post-Apartheid South Africa* (2000) ISBN 1-919798-14-5

21 *Cross-Border Raiding and Community Conflict in the Lesotho-South African Border Zone* (2001) ISBN 1-919798-16-1

22 *Immigration, Xenophobia and Human Rights in South Africa* (2001) ISBN 1-919798-30-7

23 *Gender and the Brain Drain from South Africa* (2001) ISBN 1-919798-35-8

24 *Spaces of Vulnerability: Migration and HIV/AIDS in South Africa* (2002) ISBN 1-919798-38-2

25 *Zimbabweans Who Move: Perspectives on International Migration in Zimbabwe* (2002) ISBN 1-919798-40-4

26 *The Border Within: The Future of the Lesotho-South African International Boundary* (2002) ISBN 1-919798-41-2

27 *Mobile Namibia: Migration Trends and Attitudes* (2002) ISBN 1-919798-44-7

28 *Changing Attitudes to Immigration and Refugee Policy in Botswana* (2003) ISBN 1-919798-47-1

29 *The New Brain Drain from Zimbabwe* (2003) ISBN 1-919798-48-X

30 *Regionalizing Xenophobia? Citizen Attitudes to Immigration and Refugee Policy in Southern Africa* (2004) ISBN 1-919798-53-6

31 *Migration, Sexuality and HIV/AIDS in Rural South Africa* (2004) ISBN 1-919798-63-3

32 *Swaziland Moves: Perceptions and Patterns of Modern Migration* (2004) ISBN 1-919798-67-6

33 *HIV/AIDS and Children's Migration in Southern Africa* (2004) ISBN 1-919798-70-6

34 *Medical Leave: The Exodus of Health Professionals from Zimbabwe* (2005) ISBN 1-919798-74-9

35 *Degrees of Uncertainty: Students and the Brain Drain in Southern Africa* (2005) ISBN 1-919798-84-6

36 *Restless Minds: South African Students and the Brain Drain* (2005) ISBN 1-919798-82-X

37 *Understanding Press Coverage of Cross-Border Migration in Southern Africa since 2000* (2005) ISBN 1-919798-91-9

38 *Northern Gateway: Cross-Border Migration Between Namibia and Angola* (2005) ISBN 1-919798-92-7

39 *Early Departures: The Emigration Potential of Zimbabwean Students* (2005) ISBN 1-919798-99-4

40 *Migration and Domestic Workers: Worlds of Work, Health and Mobility in Johannesburg* (2005) ISBN 1-920118-02-0

41 *The Quality of Migration Services Delivery in South Africa* (2005) ISBN 1-920118-03-9

42 *States of Vulnerability: The Future Brain Drain of Talent to South Africa* (2006) ISBN 1-920118-07-1

43 *Migration and Development in Mozambique: Poverty, Inequality and Survival* (2006) ISBN 1-920118-10-1

44 *Migration, Remittances and Development in Southern Africa* (2006) ISBN 1-920118-15-2

45 *Medical Recruiting: The Case of South African Health Care Professionals* (2007) ISBN 1-920118-47-0

46 *Voices From the Margins: Migrant Women's Experiences in Southern Africa* (2007) ISBN 1-920118-50-0

47 *The Haemorrhage of Health Professionals From South Africa: Medical Opinions* (2007) ISBN 978-1-920118-63-1

48 *The Quality of Immigration and Citizenship Services in Namibia* (2008) ISBN 978-1-920118-67-9

49 *Gender, Migration and Remittances in Southern Africa* (2008) ISBN 978-1-920118-70-9

50 *The Perfect Storm: The Realities of Xenophobia in Contemporary South Africa* (2008) ISBN 978-1-920118-71-6

51 *Migrant Remittances and Household Survival in Zimbabwe* (2009) ISBN 978-1-920118-92-1

52 *Migration, Remittances and 'Development' in Lesotho* (2010) ISBN 978-1-920409-26-5

53 *Migration-Induced HIV and AIDS in Rural Mozambique and Swaziland* (2011) ISBN 978-1-920409-49-4

54 *Medical Xenophobia: Zimbabwean Access to Health Services in South Africa* (2011) ISBN 978-1-920409-63-0

55 *The Engagement of the Zimbabwean Medical Diaspora* (2011) ISBN 978-1-920409-64-7

56 *Right to the Classroom: Educational Barriers for Zimbabweans in South Africa* (2011) ISBN 978-1-920409-68-5

57 *Patients Without Borders: Medical Tourism and Medical Migration in Southern Africa* (2012) ISBN 978-1-920409-74-6

58 *The Disengagement of the South African Medical Diaspora* (2012) ISBN 978-1-920596-00-2

59 *The Third Wave: Mixed Migration from Zimbabwe to South Africa* (2012) ISBN 978-1-920596-01-9

60 *Linking Migration, Food Security and Development* (2012) ISBN 978-1-920596-02-6

61 *Unfriendly Neighbours: Contemporary Migration from Zimbabwe to Botswana* (2012) ISBN 978-1-920596-16-3

62 *Heading North: The Zimbabwean Diaspora in Canada* (2012) ISBN 978-1-920596-03-3

63 *Dystopia and Disengagement: Diaspora Attitudes Towards South Africa* (2012) ISBN 978-1-920596-04-0

64 *Soft Targets: Xenophobia, Public Violence and Changing Attitudes to Migrants in South Africa after May 2008* (2013) ISBN 978-1-920596-05-7

65 *Brain Drain and Regain: Migration Behaviour of South African Medical Professionals* (2014) ISBN 978-1-920596-07-1

66 *Xenophobic Violence in South Africa: Denialism, Minimalism, Realism* (2014) ISBN 978-1-920596-08-8

67 *Migrant Entrepreneurship Collective Violence and Xenophobia in South Africa* (2014) ISBN 978-1-920596-09-5

68 *Informal Migrant Entrepreneurship and Inclusive Growth in South Africa, Zimbabwe and Mozambique* (2015) ISBN 978-1-920596-10-1

69 *Calibrating Informal Cross-Border Trade in Southern Africa* (2015) ISBN 978-1-920596-13-2

Printed in the United States
By Bookmasters